The spirits of truth and falsehood
Struggle within the heart of man;
Truth born out of the spring of Light,
Falsehood from the well of darkness.
And according as a man inherits truth
So will he avoid darkness.

—from the Manual of Discipline
of the Dead Sea Scrolls

THE ESSENE GOSPEL OF PEACE

BOOK ONE*

*The Third Century Aramaic Manuscript
and Old Slavonic Texts
Compared, Edited and Translated by*

EDMOND BORDEAUX SZEKELY

MCMLXXXI
INTERNATIONAL BIOGENIC SOCIETY

*In spite of ever-increasing printing and publishing costs, for the last fifty years the price of this volume has been maintained at $1.00, thanks to the generosity of the founder of the *International Biogenic Society,* who considered that the extremely important message contained in these pages should always be made permanently available to everyone.

SOME BOOKS BY EDMOND BORDEAUX SZEKELY

THE ESSENE WAY—BIOGENIC LIVING
THE ESSENE GOSPEL OF PEACE, BOOK ONE
BOOK TWO, THE UNKNOWN BOOKS OF THE ESSENES
BOOK THREE, LOST SCROLLS OF THE ESSENE BROTHERHOOD
BOOK FOUR, THE TEACHINGS OF THE ELECT
THE DISCOVERY OF THE ESSENE GOSPEL: The Essenes & the Vatican
SEARCH FOR THE AGELESS, in Three Volumes
THE ESSENE BOOK OF CREATION
THE ESSENE JESUS
THE ESSENE BOOK OF ASHA
THE ZEND AVESTA OF ZARATHUSTRA
ARCHEOSOPHY, A NEW SCIENCE
THE ESSENE ORIGINS OF CHRISTIANITY
TEACHINGS OF THE ESSENES FROM ENOCH TO THE DEAD SEA SCROLLS
THE ESSENES, BY JOSEPHUS AND HIS CONTEMPORARIES
THE ESSENE TEACHINGS OF ZARATHUSTRA
THE ESSENE SCIENCE OF LIFE
THE ESSENE CODE OF LIFE
THE ESSENE SCIENCE OF FASTING AND THE ART OF SOBRIETY
ESSENE COMMUNIONS WITH THE INFINITE
THE FIRST ESSENE
THE BIOGENIC REVOLUTION
THE ORIGIN OF LIFE
THE COSMOTHERAPY OF THE ESSENES
THE LIVING BUDDHA
SIDDARTHA, THE PILGRIM
PILGRIM OF THE HIMALAYAS
MAN IN THE COSMIC OCEAN
TOWARD THE CONQUEST OF THE INNER COSMOS
FATHER, GIVE US ANOTHER CHANCE
THE ECOLOGICAL HEALTH GARDEN, THE BOOK OF SURVIVAL
THE TENDER TOUCH: BIOGENIC FULFILLMENT
THE DIALECTICAL METHOD OF THINKING
THE EVOLUTION OF HUMAN THOUGHT
THE SOUL OF ANCIENT MEXICO
ANCIENT AMERICA: PARADISE LOST
MESSENGERS FROM ANCIENT CIVILIZATIONS
SEXUAL HARMONY: THE NEW EUGENICS
LUDWIG VAN BEETHOVEN, PROMETHEUS OF THE MODERN WORLD
THE FIERY CHARIOTS
CREATIVE WORK: KARMA YOGA
THE ART OF STUDY: THE SORBONNE METHOD
COSMOS, MAN AND SOCIETY
THE BOOK OF LIVING FOODS
SCIENTIFIC VEGETARIANISM
THE CONQUEST OF DEATH

Book Design by Golondrina Graphics

FOREWORD

Nearly two thousand years have passed since the Son of Man taught the way, the truth and the life of mankind. He brought health to the sick, wisdom to the ignorant and happiness to those in misery. He conquered half of humanity and the whole of the civilization of the West. This fact proves the eternal vitality of the Master's words, and their supreme and incomparable value.

The content of this book represents only about a third of the complete manuscripts which exist in Aramaic in the Secret Archives of the Vatican and in old Slavonic in the Royal Archives of the Habsburgs (now the property of the Austrian Government).

We owe the existence of these two versions to the Nestorian priests who, under pressure of the advancing hordes of Genghis Khan, were forced to flee from the East towards the West, bearing all their ancient scriptures and ikons with them.

The ancient Aramaic texts date from the 3rd century after Christ, while the old Slavonic version is a literal translation of the former. Exactly how the texts traveled from Palestine to the interior of Asia into the hands of the Nestorian priests, archeologists are not yet able to reconstruct for us.

We have nothing to add to this text. It speaks for itself. The reader who studies the pages that follow with concentration, will feel the eternal vitality and powerful evidence of these profound truths which mankind needs today more urgently than ever before.

"And the truth shall bear witness of itself."

London, 1937.

EDMOND BORDEAUX SZEKELY

Preface to the Golden Anniversary (1978) Edition

Fifty years have passed since the first publication of Book One of the *Essene Gospel of Peace,* as well as the founding of the *International Biogenic Society,* dedicated to the all-sided application of the ageless Essene Teachings in our daily lives in the twentieth century. In that time, the world has undergone a devastating global war and once again faces seemingly insurmountable problems in the form of planetary pollution, food and energy shortage, and growing tensions between political philosophies. And still these timeless words of Jesus continue to sow their seeds of peace and love in a troubled world. Over ten million readers have absorbed the message of the Essene Gospel since 1928, and their numbers grow daily. Victor Hugo said, "There is no greater power than that of an idea whose time has come." Perhaps the idea of the simple strength of the Essene philosophy has finally come. Perhaps it is not yet too late for the transforming power of these words of Jesus, in their original purity and simplicity, to work its magic on a world which needs it as never before in history.

After more than forty years of extensive research concerning events which transformed the whole history of our planet, the serious seeker of truth may now read, in addition to this Book One, its sequels, *Book Two: The Unknown Books of the Essenes,* and *Book Three: Lost Scrolls of the Essene Brotherhood.* *

In 1975, a major event took place: the long-awaited publication of *The Discovery of the Essene Gospel of Peace* — a book which finally answers the questions regarding the Essene Gospel addressed to us during the last half century from all over the world. Volume One of *Search for the Ageless,* published in 1977, also sheds light on the amazing history of the Essene Gospel, and Volume Two, *The Great Experiment,* tells of the wildfire growth of the Essene-Biogenic movement, a spiritual renaissance taking place all over the world within the framework of the International Biogenic Society. Volume Three, *The Chemistry of Youth,* correlates the thousands of facts and discoveries in modern medical research and biochemistry. And the all-encompassing textbook of the International Biogenic Society, *The Essene Way-Biogenic Living,* verifies the eternal principles of the Essene Gospel of Peace, giving concrete, practical instructions on how to apply them in our daily lives in the twentieth century. Now in a newly improved, enlarged edition (it first appeared in 1928 in France as *La Vie Biogenique*), this "Essene Encyclopedia" has reached a popularity second only to this volume with readers all over the world.

EDMOND BORDEAUX SZEKELY

Book Four: The Teachings of the Elect was published posthumously in 1981.

"They sent out healers. And one of these was Jesus, the Essene. He walked among the sick and the troubled, and he brought them the knowledge they needed to cure themselves. Some who followed him wrote down what passed between him and those who suffered and were heavy-laden. The Elders of the Brotherhood made poetry of the words, and made unforgettable the story of the Healer of Men, the Good Shepherd. And when the time came at last for the Brothers to leave the desert and go to another place, the scrolls stayed behind as buried sentinels, as forgotten guardians of eternal and living truth.

A dark age began, a time of savagery, of barbarism, of book-burning, of superstition and worship of empty idols. The gentle Jesus was lost forever in the image of a crucified God; the Essene brothers hid their teachings in the minds of the few who could preserve them for their descendants, and the Scrolls of Healing lay neglected beneath the shifting shadows of the desert. . ."

—*The Discovery of the Essene Gospel of Peace*, by Edmond Bordeaux Szekely

And then many sick and maimed came to Jesus, asking him: "If you know all things, tell us, why do we suffer with these grievous plagues? Why are we not whole like other men? Master, heal us, that we too may be made strong, and need abide no longer in our misery. We know that you have it in your power to heal all manner of disease. Free us from Satan and from all his great afflictions. Master, have compassion on us."

And Jesus answered: "Happy are you, that you hunger for the truth, for I will satisfy you with the bread of wisdom. Happy are you, that you knock, for I will open to you the door of life. Happy are you, that you would cast off the power of Satan, for I will lead you into the kingdom of our Mother's angels, where the power of Satan cannot enter."

And they asked him in amazement: "Who is our Mother and which her angels? And where is her kingdom?"

"Your Mother is in you, and you in her. She bore you: she gives you life. It was she who gave to you your body, and to her shall you one day give it back again. Happy are you when you come to know her and her kingdom; if you receive your Mother's angels and if you do her laws. I tell you truly, he who does these things shall never see disease. For the power of our Mother is above all. And it destroys Satan and his kingdom, and has rule over all your bodies and all living things.

"The blood which runs in us is born of the blood of our Earthly Mother. Her blood falls from the clouds; leaps up from the womb of the earth; babbles in the brooks of the mountains; flows wide in the rivers of the plains; sleeps in the lakes; rages mightily in tempestuous seas.

"The air which we breathe is born of the breath of our Earthly Mother. Her breath is azure in the heights of the heavens; soughs in the tops of the mountains; whispers in the leaves of the forest; billows over the cornfields; slumbers in the deep valleys; burns hot in the desert.

"The hardness of our bones is born of the bones of our Earthly Mother, of the rocks and of the stones. They stand naked to the heavens on the tops of mountains; are as giants that lie sleeping on the sides of the mountains, as idols set in the desert, and are hidden in the deepness of the earth.

"The tenderness of our flesh is born of the flesh of our Earthly Mother; whose flesh waxes yellow and red in the fruits of the trees, and nurtures us in the furrows of the fields.

"Our bowels are born of the bowels of our Earthly Mother, and are hid from our eyes, like the invisible depths of the earth.

"The light of our eyes, the hearing of our ears, both are born of the colors and the sounds of our Earthly Mother; which enclose us about, as the waves of the sea a fish, as the eddying air a bird.

"I tell you in very truth, Man is the Son of the Earthly Mother, and from her did the Son of Man receive his whole body, even as the body of the newborn babe is born of the womb of his mother. I tell you truly, you are one with the Earthly Mother; she is in you, and you in her. Of her were you born, in her do you live, and to her shall you return again. Keep, therefore, her laws, for none can live long, neither be happy, but he who honors his Earthly Mother and does her laws. For your breath is her breath; your blood her blood; your bone her bone; your flesh her flesh; your bowels her bowels; your eyes and your ears are her eyes and her ears.

"I tell you truly, should you fail to keep but one only of all these laws, should you harm but one only of all your body's members, you shall be utterly lost in your grievous sickness, and there shall be weeping and gnashing of teeth. I tell you, unless you follow the laws of your Mother, you can in no wise escape death. And he who clings to the laws of his Mother, to him shall his Mother cling also. She shall heal all his plagues, and he shall never become sick. She gives him long life, and protects him from all afflictions; from fire, from water, from the bite of venomous serpents. For your Mother bore you, keeps life within you. She has given you her body, and none but she heals you. Happy is he who loves his Mother and lies quietly in her bosom. For your Mother loves you, even when you turn away from her. And how much more shall she love you, if you turn to her again? I tell you truly, very great is her love, greater than the greatest of mountains, deeper than the deepest seas. And those who love their Mother, she never deserts them. As the hen protects her chickens, as the lioness her cubs, as the mother her newborn babe, so does the Earthly Mother protect the Son of Man from all danger and from all evils.

"For I tell you truly, evils and dangers innumerable lie in wait for the Sons of Men. Beelzebub, the prince of all devils, the source of every evil, lies in wait in the body of all the Sons of Men. He is death, the lord of every plague, and taking upon him a pleasing raiment, he tempts and entices the Sons of Men. Riches does he promise, and power, and splendid palaces, and garments of gold and silver, and a multitude of servants, all these; he promises renown and glory, fornication and lustfulness, gluttony and wine-bibbing, riotous living, and slothfulness and idle days. And he entices every one by that to which their heart is most inclined. And in the day that the Sons of Men have already become the slaves of all these vanities and abominations, then in payment thereof he snatches from the Sons of Men all those things which the Earthly Mother gave them so abundantly. He takes from them their breath, their blood, their bone, their flesh, their bowels, their eyes and their ears. And the breath of the Son of Man becomes short and stifled, full of pain and evil-smelling, like the breath of unclean beasts. And his blood becomes thick and evil-smelling, like the water of the swamps; it clots and blackens, like the night of death. And his bone becomes hard and knotted; it melts away within and breaks asunder, as a stone falling down upon a rock. And his flesh waxes fat and watery; it rots and putrefies, with scabs and boils that are an abomination.

And his bowels become full with abominable filthiness, with oozing streams of decay; and multitudes of abominable worms have their habitation there. And his eyes grow dim, till dark night enshrouds them, and his ears become stopped, like the silence of the grave. And last of all shall the erring Son of Man lose life. For he kept not the laws of his Mother, and added sin to sin. Therefore, are taken from him all the gifts of the Earthly Mother: breath, blood, bone, flesh, bowels, eyes and ears, and after all else, life, with which the Earthly Mother crowned his body.

"But if the erring Son of Man be sorry for his sins and undo them, and return again to his Earthly Mother; and if he do his Earthly Mother's laws and free himself from Satan's clutches, resisting his temptations, then does the Earthly Mother receive again her erring Son with love and sends him her angels that they may serve him. I tell you truly, when the Son of Man resists the Satan that dwells in him and does not his will, in the same hour are found the Mother's angels there, that they may serve him with all their power and free utterly the Son of Man from the power of Satan.

"For no man can serve two masters. For either he serves Beelzebub and his devils or else he serves our Earthly Mother and her angels. Either he serves death or he serves life. I tell you truly, happy are those that do the laws of life and wander not upon the paths of death. For in them the forces of life wax strong and they escape the plagues of death."

And all those round about him listened to his words with amazement, for his word was with power, and he taught quite otherwise than the priests and scribes.

And though the sun was now set, they departed not to their homes. They sat round about Jesus and asked him: "Master, which are these laws of life? Rest with us awhile longer and teach us. We would listen to your teaching that we may be healed and become righteous."

And Jesus himself sat down in their midst and said: "I tell you truly, none can be happy, except he do the Law."

And the others answered: "We all do the laws of Moses,

our lawgiver, even as they are written in the holy scriptures."

And Jesus answered: "Seek not the law in your scriptures, for the law is life, whereas the scripture is dead. I tell you truly, Moses received not his laws from God in writing, but through the living word. The law is living word of living God to living prophets for living men. In everything that is life is the law written. You find it in the grass, in the tree, in the river, in the mountain, in the birds of heaven, in the fishes of the sea; but seek it chiefly in yourselves. For I tell you truly, all living things are nearer to God than the scripture which is without life. God so made life and all living things that they might by the everlasting word teach the laws of the true God to man. God wrote not the laws in the pages of books, but in your heart and in your spirit. They are in your breath, your blood, your bone; in your flesh, your bowels, your eyes, your ears, and in every little part of your body. They are present in the air, in the water, in the earth, in the plants, in the sunbeams, in the depths and in the heights. They all speak to you that you may understand the tongue and the will of the living God. But you shut your eyes that you may not see, and you shut your ears that you may not hear. I tell you truly, that the scripture is the work of man, but life and all its hosts are the work of our God. Wherefore do you not listen to the words of God which are written in His works? And wherefore do you study the dead scriptures which are the work of the hands of men?"

"How may we read the laws of God elsewhere than in the scriptures? Where are they written? Read them to us from there where you see them, for we know nothing else but the scriptures which we have inherited from our forefathers. Tell us the laws of which you speak, that hearing them we may be healed and justified."

Jesus said: "You do not understand the words of life, because you are in death. Darkness darkens your eyes and your ears are stopped with deafness. For I tell you, it profits you not at all that you pore over dead scriptures if by your deeds you deny him who has given you the scriptures.

I tell you truly, God and his laws are not in that which you do. They are not in gluttony and in wine-bibbing, neither in riotous living, nor in lustfulness, nor in seeking after riches, nor yet in hatred of your enemies. For all these things are far from the true God and from his angels. But all these things come from the kingdom of darkness and the lord of all evils. And all these things do you carry in yourselves; and so the word and the power of God enter not into you, because all manner of evil and all manner of abominations have their dwelling in your body and your spirit. If you will that the living God's word and his power may enter you, defile not your body and your spirit; for the body is the temple of the spirit, and the spirit is the temple of God. Purify, therefore, the temple, that the Lord of the temple may dwell therein and occupy a place that is worthy of him.

"And from all temptations of your body and your spirit, coming from Satan, withdraw beneath the shadow of God's heaven.

"Renew yourselves and fast. For I tell you truly, that Satan and his plagues may only be cast out by fasting and by prayer. Go by yourself and fast alone, and show your fasting to no man. The living God shall see it and great shall be your reward. And fast till Beelzebub and all his evils depart from you, and all the angels of our Earthly Mother come and serve you. For I tell you truly, except you fast, you shall never be freed from the power of Satan and from all diseases that come from Satan. Fast and pray fervently, seeking the power of the living God for your healing. While you fast, eschew the Sons of Men and seek our Earthly Mother's angels, for he that seeks shall find.

"Seek the fresh air of the forest and of the fields, and there in the midst of them shall you find the angel of air. Put off your shoes and your clothing and suffer the angel of air to embrace all your body. Then breathe long and deeply, that the angel of air may be brought within you. I tell you truly, the angel of air shall cast out of your body all uncleannesses which defiled it without and within. And thus shall all

14

evil-smelling and unclean things rise out of you, as the smoke of fire curls upwards and is lost in the sea of the air. For I tell you truly, holy is the angel of air, who cleanses all that is unclean and makes all evil-smelling things of a sweet odor. No man may come before the face of God, whom the angel of air lets not pass. Truly, all must be born again by air and by truth, for your body breathes the air of the Earthly Mother, and your spirit breathes the truth of the Heavenly Father.

"After the angel of air, seek the angel of water. Put off your shoes and your clothing and suffer the angel of water to embrace all your body. Cast yourselves wholly into his enfolding arms, and as often as you move the air with your breath, move with your body the water also. I tell you truly, the angel of water shall cast out of your body all uncleannesses which defiled it without and within. And all unclean and evil-smelling things shall flow out of you, even as the uncleannesses of garments washed in water flow away and are lost in the stream of the river. I tell you truly, holy is the angel of water who cleanses all that is unclean and makes all evil-smelling things of a sweet odor. No man may come before the face of God whom the angel of water lets not pass. In very truth, all must be born again of water and of truth, for your body bathes in the river of earthly life, and your spirit bathes in the river of life everlasting. For you receive your blood from our Earthly Mother and the truth from our Heavenly Father.

"Think not that it is sufficient that the angel of water embrace you outwards only. I tell you truly, the uncleanness within is greater by much than the uncleanness without. And he who cleanses himself without, but within remains unclean, is like to tombs that outwards are painted fair, but are within full of all manner of horrible uncleannesses and abominations. So I tell you truly, suffer the angel of water to baptize you also within, that you may become free from all your past sins, and that within likewise you may become as pure as the river's foam sporting in the sunlight.

"Seek, therefore, a large trailing gourd, having a stalk the length of a man; take out its inwards and fill it with water from the river which the sun has warmed. Hang it upon the branch of a tree, and kneel upon the ground before the angel of water, and suffer the end of the stalk of the trailing gourd to enter your hinder parts, that the water may flow through all your bowels. Afterwards rest kneeling on the ground before the angel of water and pray to the living God that he will forgive you all your past sins, and pray the angel of water that he will free your body from every uncleanness and disease. Then let the water run out from your body, that it may carry away from within it all the unclean and evil-smelling things of Satan. And you shall see with your eyes and smell with your nose all the abominations and uncleannesses which defiled the temple of your body; even all the sins which abode in your body, tormenting you with all manner of pains. I tell you truly, baptism with water frees you from all of these. Renew your baptizing with water on every day of your fast, till the day when you see that the water which flows out of you is as pure as the river's foam. Then betake your body to the coursing river, and there in the arms of the angel of water render thanks to the living God that he has freed you from your sins. And this holy baptizing by the angel of water is: Rebirth unto the new life. For your eyes shall henceforth see, and your ears shall hear. Sin no more, therefore, after your baptism, that the angels of air and of water may eternally abide in you and serve you evermore.

"And if afterward there remain within you aught of your past sins and uncleannesses, seek the angel of sunlight. Put off your shoes and your clothing and suffer the angel of sunlight to embrace all your body. Then breathe long and deeply, that the angel of sunlight may be brought within you. And the angel of sunlight shall cast out of your body all evil-smelling and unclean things which defiled it without and within. And all unclean and evil-smelling things shall rise from you, even as the darkness of night fades before the brightness of the rising sun. For I tell you truly, holy is the angel of sunlight who cleans out all uncleannesses and makes all evil-smelling things of a sweet odor. None may come before the face of God, whom the angel of sunlight lets not pass. Truly, all must be born again of sun and of truth, for your body basks in the sunlight of the Earthly Mother, and your spirit basks in the sunlight of the truth of the Heavenly Father.

"The angels of air and of water and of sunlight are brethren. They were given to the Son of Man that they might serve him, and that he might go always from one to the other.

"Holy, likewise, is their embrace. They are indivisible children of the Earthly Mother, so do not you put asunder those whom earth and heaven have made one. Let these three brother angels enfold you every day and let them abide with you through all your fasting.

"For I tell you truly, the power of devils, all sins and uncleannesses shall depart in haste from that body which is embraced by these three angels. As thieves flee from a deserted house at the coming of the lord of the house, one by the door, one by the window, and the third by the roof, each where he is found, and whither he is able, even so shall flee from your bodies all devils of evil, all past sins, and all uncleannesses and diseases which defiled the temple of your bodies. When the Earthly Mother's angels enter into your bodies, in such wise that the lords of the temple repossess it again, then shall all evil smells depart in haste by your breath and by your skin, corrupt waters by your mouth and by your skin, by your hinder and your privy parts. And all these things you shall see with your eyes and smell with your nose and touch with your hands. And when all sins and uncleannesses are gone from your body, your blood shall become as pure as our Earthly Mother's blood and as the river's foam sporting in the sunlight. And your breath shall become as pure as the breath of odorous flowers; your flesh as pure as the flesh of fruits reddening upon the leaves of trees; the light of your eye as clear and bright as the brightness of the sun shining upon the blue sky. And now shall all the angels of the Earthly Mother serve you. And your breath, your blood, your flesh shall be one with the breath, the blood and the flesh of the Earthly Mother, that your spirit also may become one with the spirit of your Heavenly Father. For truly, no one can reach the Heavenly Father unless through the Earthly Mother. Even as no newborn babe can understand the teaching of his father till his mother has suckled him, bathed him, nursed him, put him to sleep and nurtured him. While the child is yet small, his place is with his mother and he must obey his mother. When the child is grown up, his father takes him to work at his side in the field, and the child comes back to his mother only when the hour of dinner and supper is come. And now his father teaches him, that he may become skilled in the works of his father. And when the father sees that his son understands his teaching and does his work well, he gives him all his possessions, that they may belong to his beloved son, and that his son may continue his father's work. I tell you truly, happy is that son who accepts the counsel of his mother and walks therein. And a hundred times more happy is that son who accepts and walks also in the counsel of his father, for it was said to you: 'Honor thy father and thy mother that thy days may be long upon this earth.' But I say to you, Sons of Man: Honor your Earthly Mother and keep all her laws, that your days may be long on this earth, and honor your Heavenly Father that Eternal Life may be yours in the heavens. For the Heavenly Father is a hundred times greater than all fathers by seed and by blood, and greater is the Earthly Mother than all mothers by the body. And dearer is the Son of Man in the eyes of his Heavenly Father and of his Earthly Mother than are children in the eyes of their fathers by seed and by blood and of their mothers by the body. And more wise are the words and laws of your Heavenly Father and of your Earthly Mother than the words and the will of all fathers by seed and by blood, and of all mothers by the body. And of more worth also is the inheritance of your Heavenly Father and of your Earthly Mother, the everlasting kingdom of earthly and heavenly life, than all the inheritances of your fathers by seed and by blood, and of your mothers by the body.

"And your true brothers are all those who do the will of your Heavenly Father and of your Earthly Mother, and not your brothers by blood. I tell you truly, that your true brothers in the will of the Heavenly Father and of the Earthly Mother will love you a thousand times more than your brothers by blood. For since the days of Cain and Abel, when brothers by blood transgressed the will of God, there is no true brotherhood by blood. And brothers do unto brothers as do strangers. Therefore, I say to you, love your true brothers in the will of God a thousand times more than your brothers by blood.

FOR YOUR HEAVENLY FATHER IS LOVE.
FOR YOUR EARTHLY MOTHER IS LOVE.
FOR THE SON OF MAN IS LOVE.

"It is by love that the Heavenly Father and the Earthly Mother and the Son of Man become one. For the spirit of the Son of Man was created from the spirit of the Heavenly Father, and his body from the body of the Earthly Mother. Become, therefore, perfect as the spirit of your Heavenly Father and the body of your Earthly Mother are perfect. And so love your Heavenly Father, as he loves your spirit. And so love your Earthly Mother, as she loves your body. And so love your true brothers, as your Heavenly Father and your Earthly Mother love them. And then your Heavenly Father shall give you his holy spirit, and your Earthly Mother shall give you her holy body. And then shall the Sons of Men like true brothers give love one to another, the love which they received from their Heavenly Father and from their Earthly Mother; and they shall all become comforters one of another. And then shall disappear from the earth all evil and all sorrow, and there shall be love and joy upon earth. And then shall the earth be like the heavens, and the kingdom of God shall come. And then shall come the Son of Man in all his glory, to inherit the kingdom of God. And then shall the Sons of Men divide their divine inheritance, the kingdom of God. For the Sons of Men live in the Heavenly Father and in the Earthly Mother, and the Heavenly Father and the Earthly Mother live in them. And then with the kingdom of God shall come the end of the times. For the Heavenly Father's love gives to all life everlasting in the kingdom of God. For love is eternal. Love is stronger than death.

"Though I speak with the tongues of men and of angels, but have not love, I am become as sounding brass or a tinkling cymbal. Though I tell what is to come, and know all secrets, and all wisdom; and though I have faith strong as the storm which lifts mountains from their seat, but have not love, I am nothing. And though I bestow all my goods to feed the poor, and give all my fire that I have received from my Father, but have not love, I am in no wise profited. Love is patient, love is kind. Love is not envious, works not evil, knows not pride; is not rude, neither selfish; is slow to anger, imagines no mischief; rejoices not in injustice, but delights in justice. Love defends all, love believes all, love hopes all, love bears all; never exhausts itself; but as for tongues they shall cease, and, as for knowledge, it shall vanish away. For we have truth in part, and error in part, but when the fulness of perfection is come, that which is in part shall be blotted out. When a man was a child he spoke as a child, understood as a child, thought as a child; but when he became a man he put away childish things. For now we see through a glass and through dark sayings. Now we know in part, but when we are come before the face of God, we shall not know in part, but even as we are taught by him. And now remain these three: faith and hope and love; but the greatest of these is love.

"And now I speak to you in the living tongue of the living God, through the holy spirit of our Heavenly Father. There is none yet among you that can understand all this of which I speak. He who expounds to you the scriptures speaks to you in a dead tongue of dead men, through his diseased and mortal body. Him, therefore, can all men understand, for all men are diseased and all are in death. No one sees the light of life. Blind man leads blind on the dark paths of sins, diseases and sufferings; and at the last all fall into the pit of death.

"I am sent to you by the Father, that I may make the light of life to shine before you. The light lightens itself and the darkness, but the darkness knows only itself, and knows not the light. I have still many things to say to you, but you cannot bear them yet. For your eyes are used to the darkness, and the full light of the Heavenly Father would make you blind. Therefore, you cannot yet understand that which I speak to you concerning the Heavenly Father who sent me to you. Follow, therefore, first, only the laws of your Earthly Mother, of which I have told you. And when her angels shall have cleansed and renewed your bodies and strengthened your eyes, you will be able to bear the light of our Heavenly Father. When you can gaze on the brightness of the noonday sun with unflinching eyes, you can then look upon the blinding light of your Heavenly Father, which is a thousand times brighter than the brightness of a thousand suns. But how should you look upon the blinding light of your Heavenly Father, when you cannot even bear the shining of the blazing sun? Believe me, the sun is as the flame of a candle beside the sun of truth of the Heavenly Father. Have but faith, therefore, and hope, and love. I tell you truly, you shall not want your reward. If you believe in my words, you believe in him who sent me, who is the lord of all, and with whom all things are possible. For what is impossible with men, all these things are possible with God. If you believe in the angels of the Earthly Mother and do her laws, your faith shall sustain you and you shall never see disease. Have hope also in the love of your Heavenly Father, for he who trusts in him shall never be deceived, nor shall he ever see death.

"Love one another, for God is love, and so shall his angels know that you walk in his paths. And then shall all the angels come before your face and serve you. And Satan with all sins, diseases and uncleannesses shall depart from your body. Go, eschew your sins; repent yourselves; baptize yourselves; that you may be born again and sin no more."

Then Jesus rose. But all else remained sitting, for every man felt the power of his words. And then the full moon appeared between the breaking clouds and folded Jesus in its brightness. And sparks flew upward from his hair, and he stood among them in the moonlight, as though he hovered in the air. And no man moved, neither was the voice of any heard. And no one knew how long a time had passed, for time stood still.

Then Jesus stretched out his hands to them and said: "Peace be with you." And so he departed, as a breath of wind sways the green of trees.

And for a long while yet the company sat still and then they woke in the silence, one man after another, like as from a long dream. But none would go, as if the words of him who had left them ever sounded in their ears. And they sat as though they listened to some wondrous music.

But at last one, as it were a little fearfully, said: "How good it is to be here." Another: "Would that this night were everlasting." And others: "Would that he might be with us always." "Of a truth he is God's messenger, for he planted hope within our hearts." And no man wished to go home, saying: "I go not home where all is dark and joyless. Why should we go home where no one loves us?"

And they spoke on this wise, for they were almost all poor, lame, blind, maimed, beggars, homeless, despised in their wretchedness, who were only borne for pity's sake in the houses where they found a few day's refuge. Even certain, who had both home and family, said: "We also will stay with you." For every man felt that the words of him who was gone bound the little company with threads invisible. And all felt that they were born again. They saw before them a shining world, even when the moon was hidden in the clouds. And in the hearts of all blossomed wondrous flowers of wondrous beauty, the flowers of joy.

And when the bright sunbeams appeared over the earth's rim, they all felt that it was the sun of the coming kingdom of God. And with joyful countenances they went forth to meet God's angels.

And many unclean and sick followed Jesus' words and sought the banks of the murmuring streams. They put off their shoes and their clothing, they fasted, and they gave up their bodies to the angels of air, of water, and of sunshine. And the Earthly Mother's angels embraced them, possessing their bodies both inwards and outwards. And all of them saw all evils, sins and uncleannesses depart in haste from them.

And the breath of some became as stinking as that which is loosed from the bowels, and some had an issue of spittle, and evil-smelling and unclean vomit rose from their inward parts. All these uncleannesses flowed by their mouths. In some, by the nose, in others by the eyes and ears. And many did have a noisome and abominable sweat come from all their body, over all their skin. And on many limbs great hot boils broke forth, from which came out uncleannesses with an evil smell, and urine flowed abundantly from their body; and in many their urine was all but dried up and became thick as the honey of bees; that of others was almost red or black, and as hard almost as the sand of rivers. And many belched stinking gases from their bowels, like the breath of devils. And their stench became so great that none could bear it.

And when they baptized themselves, the angel of water entered their bodies, and from them flowed out all the abominations and uncleannesses of their past sins, and like a falling mountain stream gushed from their bodies a multitude of hard and soft abominations. And the ground where their waters flowed was polluted, and so great became the stench that none could remain there. And the devils left their bowels in the shape of multitudinous worms which writhed in impotent rage after the angel of water had cast them out of the bowels of the Sons of Men. And then descended upon them the power of the angel of sunshine, and they perished there in their desperate writhings, trod underfoot by the angel of sunshine. And all were trembling with terror when they looked upon all these abominations of Satan, from which the angels had saved them. And they rendered thanks to God who had sent his angels for their deliverance.

And there were some whom great pains tormented, which would not depart from them; and knowing not what they should do, they resolved to send one of them to Jesus, for they greatly wished he should be with them.

And when two were gone to seek him, they saw Jesus himself approaching by the bank of the river. And their hearts were filled with hope and joy when they heard his greeting, "Peace be with you." And many were the questions that they desired to ask him, but in their astonishment they could not begin, for nothing came into their minds. Then said Jesus to them: "I come because you need me." And one cried out: "Master, we do indeed, come and free us from our pains."

And Jesus spoke to them in parables: "You are like the prodigal son, who for many years did eat and drink, and passed his days in riotousness and lechery with his friends. And every week without his father's knowledge he incurred new debts, and squandered all in a few days. And the moneylenders always lent to him, because his father possessed great riches and always paid patiently the debts of his son. And in vain did he with fair words admonish his son, for he never listened to the admonitions of his father, who besought him in vain that he would give up his debaucheries which had no end, and that he would go to his fields to watch over the labor of his servants. And the son always promised him everything if he would pay his old debts, but the next day he began again. And for more than seven years the son continued in his riotous living. But, at last, his father lost patience and no more paid to the moneylenders the debts of his son. 'If I continue always to pay,' he said, 'there will be no end to the sins of my son.' Then the moneylenders, who were deceived, in their wrath took the son into slavery that he might by his daily toil pay back to them the money which he had borrowed. And then ceased the eating and drinking and the daily excesses. From morning until night by the sweat of his face he watered the fields, and all of his limbs ached with the unaccustomed labor. And he lived upon dry bread, and had naught but his tears with which he could water it. And three days after he suffered so much from the heat and from weariness that he said to his master: 'I can work no more, for all my limbs do ache. How long would you torment me?' 'Till the day when by the labor of your hands you pay me all your debts, and when seven years are passed, you will be free.' And the desperate son answered weeping: 'But I cannot bear so much as seven days. Have pity on me, for all my limbs do burn and ache.' And the wicked creditor cried out: 'Press on with the work; if you could for seven years spend your days and your nights in riotousness, now must you work for seven years. I will not forgive you till you pay back all your debts to the uttermost drachma.' And the son, with his limbs racked with pain, went back despairing to the fields to continue his work. Already he could hardly stand upon his feet because of his weariness and of his pains, when the seventh day was come—the Sabbath day, in which no man works in the field. Then the son gathered the remnant of his strength and staggered to the house of his father. And he cast himself down at his father's feet and said: 'Father, believe me for the last time and forgive me all my offenses against you. I swear to you that I will never again live riotously and that I will be your obedient son in all things. Free me from the hands of my oppressor. Father, look upon me and upon my sick limbs, and harden not your heart.' Then tears came into his father's eyes, and he took his son in his arms, and said: 'Let us rejoice, for today a great joy is given me, because I have found again my beloved son, who was lost.' And he clothed him with his choicest raiment and all the day long they made merry. And on the morning of the morrow he gave his son a bag of silver that he might pay to his creditors all that he owed them. And when his son came back, he said to him: 'My son, do you see that it is easy, through riotous living, to incur debts for seven years, but their payment is difficult by the heavy labor of seven years.' 'Father, it is indeed hard to pay them, even for seven days.' And his father admonished him, saying: 'For this once alone has it been permitted you to pay your debts in seven days instead of seven years, the rest is forgiven you. But take heed that in the time to come you do not incur more debts. For I tell you truly, that none else but your father forgives you your debts, because you are his son. For with all else you would have had to labor hard for seven years, as it is commanded in our laws.'

" 'My father, I will henceforth be your loving and obedient son, and I will not any more incur debts, for I know that their payment is hard.'

"And he went to his father's field and watched every day over the work of his father's laborers. And he never made his laborers work hard, for he remembered his own heavy labor. And the years passed, and his father's possession increased ever more and more beneath his hand, for the blessing of his father was upon his labor. And slowly he gave back tenfold to his father all that he had squandered in the seven years. And when his father saw that his son used well his servants and all his possessions, he said to him: 'My son, I see that my possessions are in good hands. I give you all my cattle, my house, my lands and my treasures. Let all this be your heritage, continue increasing it that I may have delight in you.' And when the son had received his inheritance from his father, he forgave their debts to all his debtors who could not pay him, for he did not forget that his debt also had been forgiven when he could not pay it. And God blessed him with long life, with many children and with much riches, because he was kind to all his servants and to all his cattle."

Then Jesus turned to the sick folk and said: "I speak to you in parables that you may better understand God's word. The seven years of eating and drinking and of riotous living are the sins of the past. The wicked creditor is Satan. The debts are diseases. The heavy labor is pains. The prodigal son, he is yourselves. The payment of the debts is the casting from you of devils and diseases, and the healing of your body. The bag of silver received from the father is the liberating power of the angels. The father is God. The father's possessions are earth and heaven. The servants of the father are the angels. The father's field is the world, which is changed into the kingdom of the heavens, if the Sons of Man work thereon together with the angels of the Heavenly Father. For I tell you, it is better that the son should obey his father and keep watch over his father's servants in the field, than that he should become the debtor of the wicked creditor and toil and sweat in serfdom to repay all his debts. It is better, likewise, if the Sons of Man also obey the laws of their Heavenly Father, and work together with his angels upon his kingdom, than that they should become the debtors of Satan, the lord of death, of all sins and all diseases, and that they should suffer with pains and sweat till they have repaid all their sins. I tell you truly, great and many are your sins. Many years have you yielded to the enticings of Satan. You have been gluttonous, winebibbers and gone a-whoring, and your past debts have multiplied. And now you must repay them, and payment is difficult and hard. Be not, therefore, already impatient after the third day, like the prodigal son, but wait patiently for the seventh day which is sanctified by God, and then go with humble and obedient heart before the face of your Heavenly Father, that he may forgive you your sins and all your past debts. I tell you truly, your Heavenly Father loves you without end, for he also allows you to pay in seven days the debts of seven years. Those that owe the sins and diseases of seven years, but pay honestly and persevere till the seventh day, to them shall our Heavenly Father forgive the debts of all these seven years."

"If we sin for seven times seven years?" asked a sick man who suffered horribly. "Even in that case the Heavenly Father forgives you all your debts in seven times seven days.

"Happy are those that persevere to the end, for the devils of Satan write all your evil deeds in a book, in the book of your body and your spirit. I tell you truly, there is not one sinful deed, but it is written, even from the beginning of the world, before our Heavenly Father. For you may escape the laws made by kings, but the laws of your God, these may none of the Sons of Man escape. And when you come before the face of God, the devils of Satan bear witness against you with your deed, and God sees your sins written in the book of your body and of your spirit and is sad in his heart. But if you repent of your sins, and by fasting and prayer you seek the angels of God, then each day that you continue to fast and to pray, God's angels blot out one year of your evil deeds from the book of your body and your spirit. And when the last page is also blotted out and cleansed from all your sins, you stand before the face of God, and God rejoices in his heart and forgets all your sins. He frees you from the clutches of Satan and from suffering; he takes you within his house and commands that all his servants, all his angels serve you. Long life does he give you, and you shall never see disease. And if, thenceforward, instead of sinning, you pass your days in doing good deeds, then the angels of God shall write all your good deeds in the book of your body and of your spirit. I tell you truly, no good deed remains unwritten before God, not from the beginning of the world. For from your kings and your governors you may wait in vain for your reward, but never do your good deeds want their reward from God.

"And when you come before the face of God, his angels bear witness for you with your good deeds. And God sees your good deeds written in your bodies and in your spirits, and rejoices in his heart. He blesses your body and your spirit and all your deeds, and gives you for a heritage his earthly and heavenly kingdom, that in it you may have life everlasting. Happy is he who can enter into the kingdom of God, for he shall never see death."

And a great silence fell at his words. And those that were discouraged took new strength from his words and continued to fast and to pray. And he who had spoken the first, said to him: "I will persevere to the seventh day." And the second, likewise, said to him: "I also will persevere to the seven times seventh day."

Jesus answered them: "Happy are those that persevere to the end, for they shall inherit the earth."

And there were many sick among them tormented with grievous pains, and they hardly crawled to Jesus' feet. For they could no longer walk upon their feet. They said: "Master, we are grievously tormented with pain; tell us what we shall do." And they showed Jesus their feet in which the bones were twisted and knotted and said: "Neither the angel of air, nor of water, nor of sunshine has assuaged our pains, notwithstanding that we baptized ourselves, and do fast and pray, and follow your words in all things."

"I tell you truly, your bones will be healed. Be not discouraged, but seek for cure nigh the healer of bones, the angel of earth. For thence were your bones taken, and thither will they return."

And he pointed with his hand to where the running of the water and the sun's heat had softened to clayey mud the earth by the edge of the water. "Sink your feet in the mire, that the embrace of the angel of earth may draw out from your bones all uncleanness and all disease. And you will see Satan and your pains fly from the embrace of the angel of earth. And the knots of your bones will vanish away, and they will be straightened, and all your pains will disappear."

And the sick followed his words, for they knew that they would be healed.

And there were also other sick who suffered much from their pains, howbeit, they persisted in their fasting. And their force was spent, and great heat tormented them. And when they would have risen from their bed to go to Jesus, their heads began to turn, as if it were a gusty wind which shook them, and as oft as they tried to stand upon their feet they fell back to the ground.

Then Jesus went to them and said: "You suffer, for Satan and his diseases torment your bodies. But fear not, for their power over you will quickly end. For Satan is like a choleric neighbor who entered his neighbor's house while he was absent, intending to take his goods away to his own house. But some told the other that his enemy was ravaging within his house, and he came back to his house, running. And when the wicked neighbor, having gathered together all that pleased him, saw from afar the master of the house returning in haste, then he was very wroth that he could not take all away, and set to breaking and spoiling all that was there, to destroy all. So that even if the things might not be his, the other might have nothing. But immediately the lord of the house came in, and before the wicked neighbor fulfilled his purpose, he took him and cast him out of the house. I tell you truly, even so did Satan enter your bodies which are the habitation of God. And he took in his power all that he wished to steal: your breath, your blood, your bone, your flesh, your bowels, your eyes, and your ears. But by your fasting and your prayer, you have called back the lord of your body and his angels. And now Satan sees that the true lord of your body returns, and that it is the end of his power. Wherefore, in his wrath he gathers his strength once again, that he may destroy your bodies before the coming of the lord. It is for this that Satan torments you so grievously, for he feels that the end is come. But let not your hearts tremble, for soon will the angels of God appear, to occupy again their abodes and rededicate them as temples of God. And they will seize Satan and cast him from your bodies with all his diseases and all his uncleannesses. And happy will you be, for you will receive the reward of your steadfastness, and you will never see disease."

And there was among the sick, one that was more tormented by Satan than all the others. And his body was as parched as a skeleton, and his skin yellow as a falling leaf. He was so weak already that he could not, even upon his hands, crawl to Jesus, and cried only to him from afar: "Master, have pity on me, for never has man suffered, not from the beginning of the world, as I do suffer. I know that you are indeed sent by God, and I know that if you will, you can straightway cast out Satan from my body. Do not the angels of God obey God's messenger? Come, Master, and cast out Satan from me now, for he rages angrily within me and grievous is his torment."

And Jesus answered him: "Satan torments you thus greatly because you have already fasted many days, and you do not pay to him his tribute. You do not feed him with all the abominations with which you hitherto defiled the temple of your spirit. You torment Satan with hunger, and so in his anger he torments you also. Fear not, for I tell you, Satan will be destroyed before your body is destroyed; for while you fast and pray, the angels of God protect your body, that Satan's power may not destroy you. And the anger of Satan is impotent against the angels of God."

Then they all came to Jesus and with loud cries besought him saying: "Master, have compassion on him, for he suffers more than we all, and if you do not at once cast Satan out of him, we fear he will not live until tomorrow."

And Jesus answered them: "Great is your faith. Be it according to your faith, and you shall see soon, face to face, the frightful countenance of Satan, and the power of the Son of Man. For I will cast out from you the powerful Satan by the strength of the innocent lamb of God, the weakest creature of the Lord. For the holy spirit of God makes more powerful the weakest than the strongest."

And Jesus milked an ewe which was feeding among the grass. And he put the milk upon the sand made hot by the sun, saying: "Lo, the power of the angel of water has entered this milk. And now the power of the angel of sunshine will enter it also."

And the milk became hot by the strength of the sun.

"And now the angels of water and of sun will join with the angel of air."

·And lo, the vapor of the hot milk began to rise slowly into the air.

"Come and breathe in by your mouth the strength of the angels of water, of sunshine, and of air, that it may come into your body and cast out the Satan from you."

And the sick man whom Satan tormented did breathe within himself, deeply, the rising whitish vapor.

"Straightway will Satan leave your body, since for three days he starves and finds no food within you. He will come out of you to satisfy his hunger by the hot steaming milk, for this food finds favor in his sight. He will smell its smell, and will not be able to resist the hunger which has tormented him three days already. But the Son of Man will destroy his body, that he may torment none else again."

Then the sick man's body was seized with an ague, and he retched as though he would vomit, but he could not. And he gasped for air, for his breath was spent. And he fainted on the lap of Jesus.

"Now does Satan leave his body. See him." And Jesus pointed to the sick man's opened mouth.

And then they all saw with astonishment and terror that Satan was coming out from his mouth in the shape of an abominable worm, straight towards the steaming milk. Then Jesus took two sharp stones in his hands and crushed the head of Satan, and drew out from the sick man all the body of the monster which was almost as long as the man. When the abominable worm came out of the sick man's throat, he recovered at once his breath, and then all his pains ceased. And the others looked with terror at the abominable body of Satan.

"See, what an abominable beast you carried and nourished in your body for long years. I have cast it out of you and killed it that it may never again torment you. Give thanks to God that his angels have made you free, and sin no more, lest Satan return to you again. Let your body be henceforth a temple dedicated to your God."

And they were all amazed at his words and at his power. And they said: "Master, you are indeed God's messenger, and do know all secrets."

"And you," answered Jesus, "be true Sons of God, that you also may partake in his power and in the knowledge of all secrets. For wisdom and power can come only from the love of God. Love, therefore, your Heavenly Father and your Earthly Mother with all your heart, and with all your spirit. And serve them, that their angels may serve you also. Let all your deeds be sacrificed to God. And feed not Satan, for the wages of sin is death. But with God lies the reward of the good, his love, which is knowledge and power of eternal life."

And they all knelt down to give thanks to God for his love.

And Jesus departed, saying: "I will come again to all who persist in prayer and fasting till the seventh day. Peace be with you."

And the sick man from whom Jesus had cast out the Satan, stood up, for the strength of life had come back to him. He breathed out deeply, and his eyes became clear, for every pain had left him. And he cast himself down upon the ground where Jesus had stood, and he kissed the print of his feet and he wept.

And it was by the bed of a stream, many sick fasted and prayed with God's angels for seven days and seven nights. And great was their reward, because they followed Jesus' words. And with the passing of the seventh day, all their pains left them. And when the sun rose over the earth's rim they saw Jesus coming towards them from the mountain, with the brightness of the rising sun about his head.

"Peace be with you."

And they said no word at all, but only cast themselves down before him, and touched the hem of his garment in token of their healing.

"Give thanks not to me, but to your Earthly Mother, who sent you her healing angels. Go, and sin no more, that you may never again see disease. And let the healing angels become your guardians."

But they answered him: "Whither should we go, Master, for with you are the words of eternal life? Tell us, what are the sins which we must shun, that we may nevermore see disease?"

Jesus answered: "Be it so according to your faith," and he sat down among them, saying:

"It was said to them of old time, 'Honor thy Heavenly Father and thy Earthly Mother, and do their commandments, that thy days may be long upon the earth.' And next afterward was given this commandment, 'Thou shalt not kill,' for life is given to all by God, and that which God has given, let not man take away. For I tell you truly, from one Mother proceeds all that lives upon the earth. Therefore, he who kills, kills his brother. And from him will the Earthly Mother turn away, and will pluck from him her quickening breasts. And he will be shunned by her angels, and Satan will have his dwelling in his body. And the flesh of slain beasts in his body will become his own tomb. For I tell you truly, he who kills, kills himself, and whoso eats the flesh of slain beasts, eats of the body of death. For in his blood every drop of their blood turns to poison; in his breath their breath to stink; in his flesh their flesh to boils; in his bones their bones to chalk; in his bowels their bowels to decay; in his eyes their eyes to scales; in his ears their ears to waxy issue. And their death will become his death. For only in the service of your Heavenly Father are your debts of seven years forgiven in seven days. But Satan forgives you nothing and you must pay him for all. 'Eye for eye, tooth for tooth, hand for hand, foot for foot; burning for burning, wound for wound; life for life, death for death.' For the wages of sin is death. Kill not, neither eat the flesh of your innocent prey, lest you become the slaves of Satan. For that is the path of sufferings, and it leads unto death. But do the will of God, that his angels may serve you on the way of life. Obey, therefore, the words of God: 'Behold, I have given you every herb bearing seed, which is upon the face of all the earth, and every tree, in the which is the fruit of a tree yielding seed; to you it shall be for meat. And to every beast of the earth, and to every fowl of the air, and to everything that creepeth upon the earth, wherein there is breath of life, I give every green herb for meat. Also the milk of every thing that moveth and liveth upon earth shall be meat for you; even as the green herb have I given unto them, so I give their milk unto you. But flesh, and the blood which quickens it, shall ye not eat. And, surely, your spurting blood will I require, your blood wherein is your soul; I will require all slain beasts, and the souls of all slain men. For I the Lord thy God am a God strong and jealous, visiting the iniquity of the fathers upon the children unto the third and fourth generation of them that hate me; and showing mercy unto thousands of them that love me, and keep my commandments. Love the Lord thy God with all thy heart, and with all thy soul, and with all thy strength: this is the first and greatest commandment.' And the second is like unto it: 'Love thy neighbor as thyself.' There is none other commandment greater than these."

And after these words they all remained silent, save one, who called out: "What am I to do, Master, if I see a wild beast rend my brother in the forest? Shall I let my brother perish, or kill the wild beast? Shall not I thus transgress the law?"

And Jesus answered: "It was said to them of old time: 'All beasts that move upon the earth, all the fish of the sea, and all the fowl of the air are given into thy power.' I tell you truly, of all creatures living upon the earth, God created only man after his image. Wherefore, beasts are for man, and not man for beasts. You do not, therefore, transgress the law if you kill the wild beast to save your brother's life. For I tell you truly, man is more than the beast. But he who kills the beast without a cause, though the beast attack him not, through lust for slaughter, or for its flesh, or for its hide, or yet for its tusks, evil is the deed which he does, for he is turned into a wild beast himself. Wherefore is his end also as the end of the wild beasts."

Then another said: "Moses, the greatest in Israel, suffered our forefathers to eat the flesh of clean beasts, and forbade only the flesh of unclean beasts. Why, therefore, do you forbid us the flesh of all beasts? Which law comes from God? That of Moses, or your law?"

And Jesus answered: "God gave, by Moses, ten commandments to your forefathers. 'These commandments are hard,' said your forefathers, and they could not keep them. When Moses saw this, he had compassion on his people, and would not that they perish. And then he gave them ten times ten commandments. For he whose feet are strong as the mountain of Zion, needs no crutches; but he whose limbs do shake, gets further having crutches, than without them. And Moses said to the Lord: 'My heart is filled with sorrow, for my people will be lost. For they are without knowledge, and are not able to understand thy commandments. They are as little children who cannot yet understand their father's words. Suffer, Lord, that I give them other laws, that they may not perish. If they may not be with thee, Lord, let them not be against thee; that they may sustain themselves, and when the time has come, and they are ripe for thy words, reveal to them thy laws.' For that did Moses break the two tablets of stone whereon were written the ten commandments, and he gave them ten times ten in their stead. And of these ten times ten the Scribes and Pharisees have made a hundred times ten commandments. And they have laid unbearable burdens on your shoulders, that they themselves do not carry. For the more nigh are the commandments to God, the less do we need; and the farther they are from God, then the more do we need. Wherefore are the laws of the Pharisees and Scribes innumerable; the laws of the Son of Man seven; of the angels three; and of God one.

"Therefore, I teach you only those laws which you can understand, that you may become men, and follow the seven laws of the Son of Man. Then will the unknown angels of the Heavenly Father also reveal their laws to you, that God's holy spirit may descend upon you, and lead you to his law."

And all were astonished at his wisdom, and asked him: "Continue, Master, and teach us all the laws which we can receive."

And Jesus continued: "God commanded your forefathers: 'Thou shalt not kill.' But their heart was hardened and they killed. Then Moses desired that at least they should not kill men, and he suffered them to kill beasts. And then the heart of your forefathers was hardened yet more, and they killed men and beasts likewise. But I do say to you: Kill neither men, nor beasts, nor yet the food which goes into your mouth. For if you eat living food, the same will quicken you, but if you kill your food, the dead food will kill you also. For life comes only from life, and from death comes always death. For everything which kills your foods, kills your bodies also. And everything which kills your bodies kills your souls also. And your bodies become what your foods are, even as your spirits, likewise, become what your thoughts are. Therefore, eat not anything which fire, or frost, or water has destroyed. For burned, frozen and rotted foods will burn, freeze and rot your body also. Be not like the foolish husbandman who sowed in his ground cooked, and frozen, and rotten seeds. And the autumn came, and his fields bore nothing. And great was his distress. But be like that husbandman who sowed in his field living seed, and whose field bore living ears of wheat, paying a hundredfold for the seeds which he planted. For I tell you truly, live only by the fire of life, and prepare not your foods with the fire of death, which kills your foods, your bodies and your souls also."

"Master, where is the fire of life?" asked some of them.

"In you, in your blood, and in your bodies."

"And the fire of death?" asked others.

"It is the fire which blazes outside your body, which is hotter than your blood. With that fire of death you cook your foods in your homes and in your fields. I tell you truly, it is the same fire which destroys your foods and your bodies, even as the fire of malice, which ravages your thoughts, ravages your spirits. For your body is that which you eat, and your spirit is that which you think. Eat nothing, therefore, which a stronger fire than the fire of life has killed. Wherefore, prepare and eat all fruits of trees, and all grasses of the fields, and all milk of beasts good for eating. For all these are fed and ripened by the fire of life; all are the gift of the angels of our Earthly Mother. But eat nothing to which only the fire of death gives savor, for such is of Satan."

"How should we cook our daily bread without fire, Master?" asked some with great astonishment.

"Let the angels of God prepare your bread. Moisten your wheat, that the angel of water may enter it. Then set it in the air, that the angel of air also may embrace it. And leave it from morning to evening beneath the sun, that the angel of sunshine may descend upon it. And the blessing of the three angels will soon make the germ of life to sprout in your wheat. Then crush your grain, and make thin wafers, as did your forefathers when they departed out of Egypt, the house of bondage. Put them back again beneath the sun from its appearing, and when it is risen to its highest in the heavens, turn them over on the other side that they be embraced there also by the angel of sunshine, and leave them there until the sun be set. For the angels of water, of air, and of sunshine fed and ripened the wheat in the field, and they, likewise, must prepare also your bread. And the same sun which, with the fire of life, made the wheat to grow and ripen, must cook your bread with the same fire. For the fire of the sun gives life to the wheat, to the bread, and to the body. But the fire of death kills the wheat, the bread, and the body. And the living angels of the living God serve only living men. For God is the God of the living, and not the God of the dead.

"So eat always from the table of God: the fruits of the trees, the grain and grasses of the field, the milk of beasts, and the honey of bees. For everything beyond these is of Satan, and leads by the way of sins and of diseases unto death. But the foods which you eat from the abundant table of God give strength and youth to your body, and you will never see disease. For the table of God fed Methuselah of old, and I tell you truly, if you live even as he lived, then will the God of the living give you also long life upon the earth as was his.

"For I tell you truly, the God of the living is richer than all the rich of the earth, and his abundant table is richer than the richest table of feasting of all the rich upon the earth. Eat, therefore, all your life at the table of our Earthly Mother, and you will never see want. And when you eat at her table, eat all things even as they are found on the table of the Earthly Mother. Cook not, neither mix all things one with another, lest your bowels become as steaming bogs. For I tell you truly, this is abominable in the eyes of the Lord.

"And be not like the greedy servant, who always ate up, at the table of his lord, the portions of others. And he devoured everything himself, and mixed all together in his gluttony. And seeing that, his lord was wroth with him, and drove him from the table. And when all had ended their meal, he mixed together all that remained upon the table, and called the greedy servant to him, and said: 'Take and eat all this with the swine, for your place is with them, and not at my table.'

41

"Take heed, therefore, and defile not with all kinds of abominations the temple of your bodies. Be content with two or three sorts of food, which you will find always upon the table of our Earthly Mother. And desire not to devour all things which you see around you. For I tell you truly, if you mix together all sorts of food in your body, then the peace of your body will cease, and endless war will rage in you. And it will be blotted out even as homes and kingdoms divided against themselves work their own destruction. For your God is the God of peace, and does never help division. Arouse not, therefore, against you the wrath of God, lest he drive you from his table, and lest you be compelled to go to the table of Satan, where the fire of sins, diseases, and death will corrupt your body.

"And when you eat, never eat unto fulness. Flee the temptations of Satan, and listen to the voice of God's angels. For Satan and his power tempt you always to eat more and more. But live by the spirit, and resist the desires of the body. And your fasting is always pleasing in the eyes of the angels of God. So give heed to how much you have eaten when your body is sated, and always eat less by a third.

"Let the weight of your daily food be not less than a mina, but mark that it go not beyond two. Then will the angels of God serve you always, and you will never fall into the bondage of Satan and of his diseases. Trouble not the work of the angels in your body by eating often. For I tell you truly, he who eats more than twice in the day does in him the work of Satan. And the angels of God leave his body, and soon Satan will take possession of it. Eat only when the sun is highest in the heavens, and again when it is set. And you will never see disease, for such finds favor in the eyes of the Lord. And if you will that the angels of God rejoice in your body, and that Satan shun you afar, then sit but once in the day at the table of God. And then your days will be long upon the earth, for this is pleasing in the eyes of the Lord. Eat always when the table of God is served before you, and eat always of that which you find upon the table of God. For I tell you truly, God knows well what your body needs, and when it needs.

"From the coming of the month of Ijar, eat barley; from the month of Sivan, eat wheat, the most perfect among all seed-bearing herbs. And let your daily bread be made of wheat, that the Lord may take care of your bodies. From Tammuz, eat the sour grape, that your body may diminish and Satan may depart from it. In the month of Elul, gather the grape that the juice may serve you as drink. In the month of Marchesvan, gather the sweet grape, dried and sweetened by the angel of sun, that your bodies may increase, for the angels of the Lord dwell in them. You should eat figs rich in juice in the months of Ab and Shebat, and what remain, let the angel of sun keep them for you; eat them with the meat of almonds in all the months when the trees bear no fruits. And the herbs which come after rain, these eat in the month of Thebet, that your blood may be cleansed of all your sins. And in the same month begin to eat also the milk of your beasts, because for this did the Lord give the herbs of the fields to all the beasts which render milk, that they might with their milk feed man. For I tell you truly, happy are they that eat only at the table of God, and eschew all the abominations of Satan. Eat not unclean foods brought from far countries, but eat always that which your trees bear. For your God knows well what is needful for you, and where and when. And he gives to all peoples of all kingdoms for food that which is best for each. Eat not as the heathen do, who stuff themselves in haste, defiling their bodies with all manner of abominations.

"For the power of God's angels enters into you with the living food which the Lord gives you from his royal table. And when you eat, have above you the angel of air, and below you the angel of water. Breathe long and deeply at all your meals, that the angel of air may bless your repasts. And chew well your food with your teeth, that it become water, and that the angel of water turn it into blood in your body. And eat slowly, as it were a prayer you make to the Lord. For I tell you truly, the power of God enters into you, if you eat after this manner at his table. But Satan turns into a steaming bog the body of him upon whom the angels of air and water do not descend at his repasts. And the Lord suffers him no longer at his table. For the table of the Lord is an altar, and he who eats at the table of God is in a temple. For I tell you truly, the body of the Son of Man is turned into a temple, and his inwards into an altar, if he does the commandments of God. Wherefore, put naught upon the altar of the Lord when your spirit is vexed, neither think upon any one with anger in the temple of God. And enter only into the Lord's sanctuary when you feel in yourselves the call of his angels, for all that you eat in sorrow, or in anger, or without desire, becomes a poison in your body. For the breath of Satan defiles all these. Place with joy your offerings upon the altar of your body, and let all evil thoughts depart from you when you receive into your body the power of God from his table. And never sit at the table of God before he call you by the angel of appetite.

"Rejoice, therefore, always with God's angels at their royal table, for this is pleasing to the heart of the Lord. And your life will be long upon the earth, for the most precious of God's servants will serve you all your days: the angel of joy.

"And forget not that every seventh day is holy and consecrated to God. On six days feed your body with the gifts of the Earthly Mother, but on the seventh day sanctify your body for your Heavenly Father. On the seventh day eat not any earthly food, but live only on the words of God, and be all the day with the angels of the Lord in the kingdom of the Heavenly Father. And on the seventh day let the angels of God build the kingdom of the heavens in your body, as you labor for six days in the kingdom of the Earthly Mother. And let not food trouble the work of the angels in your body throughout the seventh day. And God will give you long life upon earth, that you may have life everlasting in the kingdom of the heavens. For I tell you truly, if you see not diseases any more upon earth, you will live for ever in the kingdom of the heavens.

"And God will send you each morning the angel of sunshine to wake you from your sleep. Therefore, obey your Heavenly Father's summons, and lie not idle in your beds, for the angels of air and water await you already without. And labor all day long with the angels of the Earthly Mother that you may come to know them and their works ever more and more well. But when the sun is set, and your Heavenly Father sends you his most precious angel, sleep, then take your rest, and be all the night with the angel of sleep. And then will your Heavenly Father send you his unknown angels, that they may be with you the livelong night. And the Heavenly Father's unknown angels will teach you many things concerning the kingdom of God, even as the angels that you know of the Earthly Mother, instruct you in the things of her kingdom. For I tell you truly, you will be every night the guests of the kingdom of your Heavenly Father, if you do his commandments. And when you wake up upon the morrow, you will feel in you the power of the unknown angels. And your Heavenly Father will send them to you every night, that they may build your spirit, even as every day the Earthly Mother sends you her angels, that they may build your body. For I tell you truly, if in the daytime your Earthly Mother folds you in her arms, and in the night the Heavenly Father breathes his kiss upon you, then will the Sons of Men become the Sons of God.

"Resist day and night the temptations of Satan. Wake not by night, neither sleep by day, lest the angels of God depart from you.

"And take no delight in any drink, nor in any smoke from Satan, waking you by night and making you to sleep by day. For I tell you truly, all the drinks and smokes of Satan are abominations in the eyes of your God.

"Commit not whoredom, by night or by day, for the whoremonger is like a tree whose sap runs out from its trunk. And that tree will be dried up before its time, nor will it ever bear fruit. Therefore, go not a-whoring, lest Satan dry up your body, and the Lord make your seed unfruitful.

"Shun all that is too hot and too cold. For it is the will of your Earthly Mother that neither heat nor cold should harm your body. And let not your bodies become either hotter or colder than as God's angels warm or cool them. And if you do the commandments of the Earthly Mother, then as oft as your body becomes too hot, will she send the angel of coolness to cool you, and as oft as your body becomes too cold, will she send you the angel of heat to warm you again.

"Follow the example of all the angels of the Heavenly Father and of the Earthly Mother, who work day and night, without ceasing, upon the kingdoms of the heavens and of the earth. Therefore, receive also into yourselves the strongest of God's angels, the angel of deeds, and work all together upon the kingdom of God. Follow the example of the running water, the wind as it blows, the rising and setting of the sun, the growing plants and trees, the beasts as they run and gambol, the wane and waxing of the moon, the stars as they come and go again; all these do move, and do perform their labors. For all which has life does move, and only that which is dead is still. And God is the God of the living, and Satan that of the dead. Serve, therefore, the living God, that the eternal movement of life may sustain you, and that you may escape the eternal stillness of death. Work, therefore, without ceasing, to build the kingdom of God, lest you be cast into the kingdom of Satan. For eternal joy abounds in the living kingdom of God, but still sorrow darkens the kingdom of death of Satan. Be, therefore, true Sons of your Earthly Mother and of your Heavenly Father, that you fall not as slaves of Satan. And your Earthly Mother and Heavenly Father will send you their angels to teach, to love, and to serve you. And their angels will write the commandments of God in your head, in your heart, and in your hands, that you may know, feel, and do God's commandments.

"And pray every day to your Heavenly Father and Earthly Mother, that your soul become as perfect as your Heavenly Father's holy spirit is perfect, and that your body become as perfect as the body of your Earthly Mother is perfect. For if you understand, feel, and do the commandments, then all for which you pray to your Heavenly Father and your Earthly Mother will be given you. For the wisdom, the love, and the power of God are above all.

"After this manner, therefore, pray to your Heavenly Father: Our Father which art in heaven, hallowed be thy name. Thy kingdom come. Thy will be done on earth as it is in heaven. Give us this day our daily bread. And forgive us our debts, as we forgive our debtors. And lead us not into temptation, but deliver us from evil. For thine is the kingdom, the power, and the glory, for ever. Amen.

"And after this manner pray to your Earthly Mother: Our Mother which art upon earth, hallowed be thy name. Thy kingdom come, and thy will be done in us, as it is in thee. As thou sendest every day thy angels, send them to us also. Forgive us our sins, as we atone all our sins against thee. And lead us not into sickness, but deliver us from all evil, for thine is the earth, the body, and the health. Amen.

And they all prayed together with Jesus to the Heavenly Father and to the Earthly Mother.

And afterwards Jesus spoke thus to them: "Even as your bodies have been reborn through the Earthly Mother's angels, may your spirit, likewise, be reborn through the angels of the Heavenly Father. Become, therefore, true Sons of your Father and of your Mother, and true Brothers of the Sons of Men. Till now you were at war with your Father, with your Mother, and with your Brothers. And you have served Satan. From today live at peace with your Heavenly Father, and with your Earthly Mother, and with your Brothers, the Sons of Men. And fight only against Satan, lest he rob you of your peace. I give the peace of your Earthly Mother to your body, and the peace of your Heavenly Father to your spirit. And let the peace of both reign among the Sons of Men.

"Come to me, all that are weary and that suffer in strife and affliction! For my peace will strengthen you and comfort you. For my peace is exceeding full of joy. Wherefore do I always greet you after this manner: 'Peace be with you!' Do you always, therefore, so greet one another, that upon your body may descend the peace of your Earthly Mother, and upon your spirit the peace of your Heavenly Father. And then you will find peace also among yourselves, for the kingdom of God is within you. And now return to your Brothers with whom hitherto you were at war, and give your peace to them also. For happy are they that strive for peace, for they will find the peace of God. Go, and sin no more. And give to every one your peace, even as I have given my peace unto you. For my peace is of God. Peace be with you."

And he left them.

And his peace descended upon them; and in their heart the angel of love, in their head the wisdom of law, and in their hands the power of rebirth, they went forth among the Sons of Men, to bring the light of peace to those that warred in darkness.

And they parted, wishing one to another:

"PEACE BE WITH YOU."

THE STORY OF THE ESSENE GOSPEL OF PEACE

Translated by Edmond Bordeaux Szekely

In Four Volumes

It was in 1928 that Edmond Bordeaux Szekely first published his translation of Book One of *The Essene Gospel of Peace,* an ancient manuscript he had found in the Secret Archives of the Vatican as the result of limitless patience, faultless scholarship, and unerring intuition. This story is told in his book, *The Discovery of the Essene Gospel of Peace,* published in 1975. The English version of Book One appeared in 1937, and ever since, the little volume has traveled over the world, appearing in many different languages, gaining every year more and more readers, until now, still with no commercial advertisement, over a million copies have been sold in the United States alone. It was not until almost fifty years after the first French translation that Book Two and Book Three appeared *(The Unknown Books of the Essenes* and *Lost Scrolls of the Essene Brotherhood),* achieving rapidly the popularity of Book One.

In 1981, Book Four, *The Teachings of the Elect,* was published posthumously according to Dr. Szekely's wishes, representing yet another fragment of the complete manuscript which exists in Aramaic in the Secret Archives of the Vatican and in old Slavonic in the Royal Library of the Habsburgs (now the property of the Austrian government). The poetic style of the translator brings to vivid reality the exquisitely beautiful words of Jesus and the Elders of the Essene Brotherhood. Some of the chapters: The Essene Communions. The Sevenfold Peace. The Holy Streams of Life, Light, and Sound. The Gift of the Humble Grass.

All four volumes of *The Essene Gospel of Peace* are available in English from the International Biogenic Society mailing address: I.B.S. Internacional, Box 849, Nelson, B.C., Canada V1L 6A5. A free descriptive catalogue of these and all the collected works of Edmond Bordeaux Szekely will be gladly sent upon request.

EXCERPTS FROM
The Essene Gospel of Peace, Book Two:
The Unknown Books of the Essenes

And one man spoke: "But, Master, we are but men, we are not angels. How then can we hope to walk in their ways? Tell us what we must do."

And Jesus spoke:

> *"As the son inherits the land of his father,*
> *So have we inherited a Holy Land*
> *From our Fathers.*
> *This land is not a field to be ploughed,*
> *But a place within us*
> *Where we may build our Holy Temple.*
> *And even as a temple must be raised,*
> *Stone by stone,*
> *So will I give to you those stones*
> *For the building of the Holy Temple;*
> *That which we have inherited*
> *From our Fathers,*
> *And their Fathers' Fathers."*

And all the men gathered around Jesus, and their faces shone with desire to hear the words which would come from his lips. And he lifted his face to the rising sun, and the radiance of its rays filled his eyes as he spoke:

> *"The Holy Temple can be built*
> *Only with the ancient Communions,*
> *Those which are spoken,*
> *Those which are thought,*
> *And those which are lived.*

For if they are spoken only with the mouth,
They are as a dead hive
Which the bees have forsaken,
That gives no more honey.
The Communions are a bridge
Between man and the angels,
And like a bridge,
Can be built only with patience,
Yea, even as the bridge over the river
Is fashioned stone by stone,
As they are found by the water's edge.

And the Communions are fourteen in number,
As the Angels of the Heavenly Father
Number seven,
And the Angels of the Earthly Mother
Number seven.
And just as the roots of the tree
Sink into the earth and are nourished,
And the branches of the tree
Raise their arms to heaven,
So is man like the trunk of the tree,
With his roots deep
In the breast of his Earthly Mother,
And his soul ascending
To the bright stars of his Heavenly Father.
And the roots of the tree
Are the Angels of the Earthly Mother,
And the branches of the tree
Are the Angels of the Heavenly Father.
And this is the sacred Tree of Life
Which stands in the Sea of Eternity.

The Essene Gospel of Peace, Book Three:
Lost Scrolls of the Essene Brotherhood

For the earth shall be filled
with the Peace of the Heavenly Father,
as the waters cover the sea.

I will invoke the Angel of Peace,
Whose breath is friendly,
Whose hand is clothed in power.
In the reign of Peace, there is neither hunger nor thirst,
Neither cold wind nor hot wind,
Neither old age nor death.
In the reign of Peace,
Both animals and men shall be undying,
Waters and plants shall be undrying,
And the food of life shall be never-failing.
It is said that the mountains
Shall bring peace to the people,
And the little hills, righteousness.
There shall be peace
As long as the sun and moon endure,
Throughout all generations.
Peace shall come down like rain upon mown grass,
As showers that water the earth.
In the reign of Peace shall the Law grow strong,
And the Children of Light shall have dominion
From sea to sea, unto the ends of the earth.
The reign of Peace hath its source
In the Heavenly Father;

By his strength he setteth fast the mountains,
He maketh the outgoings of morning and evening
To rejoice in the Light,
He bringeth to earth the river of the Law,
To water and enrich it,
He maketh soft the earth with showers;
They drop upon the pastures of the wilderness,
And the little hills rejoice on every side.
The pastures are clothed with flocks;
The valleys also are covered over with corn;
They shout for joy, they also sing.
O Heavenly Father!
Bring unto thy earth the reign of Peace!
Then shall we remember the words
Of him who taught of old the Children of Light:
I give the peace of thy Earthly Mother
To thy body,
And the peace of thy Heavenly Father
To thy spirit.
And let the peace of both
Reign among the sons of men.
Come to me all that are weary,
And that suffer in strife and affliction!
For my peace will strengthen thee and comfort thee.
For my peace is exceeding full of joy.
Wherefore do I always greet thee after this manner:
Peace be with thee!
Do thou always, therefore, so greet one another,
That upon thy body may descend
The Peace of thy Earthly Mother,
And upon thy spirit
The Peace of thy Heavenly Father.

And then wilt thou find peace also among thyselves,
For the Kingdom of the Law is within thee.
And return to thy Brothers
And give thy peace to them also,
For happy are they that strive for peace,
For they will find the peace of the Heavenly Father.
And give to every one thy peace,
Even as I have given my peace unto thee.
For my peace is of God.
Peace be with thee!

THE HOLY STREAMS

Into the innermost circle have you come, into the mystery of mysteries, that which was old when our father Enoch was young and walked the earth. Around and around have you come on your journey of many years, always following the path of righteousness, living according to the Holy Law and the sacred vows of our Brotherhood, and you have made of your body a holy temple wherein dwell the angels of God. Many years have you shared the daylight hours with the angels of the Earthly Mother; many years have you slept in the arms of the Heavenly Father, taught by his unknown angels. You have learned that the laws of the Son of Man are seven, of the angels three, and of God, one. Now you shall know of the three laws of the angels, the mystery of the three Holy Streams and the ancient way to traverse them; so shall you bathe in the light of heaven and at last behold the revelation of the mystery of mysteries: the law of God, which is One.

Now in the hour before the rising of the sun, just before the angels of the Earthly Mother breathe life into the still sleeping earth, then do you enter into the Holy Stream of Life. It is your Brother Tree who holds the mystery of this Holy Stream, and it is your Brother Tree that you will embrace in your thought, even as by day you embrace him in greeting when you walk along the lake shore. And you shall be one with the tree, for in the beginning of the times so did we all share in the Holy Stream of Life that gave birth to all creation. And as you embrace your Brother Tree, the power of the Holy Stream of Life will fill your whole body, and you will tremble before its might. Then breathe deeply of the angel of air, and say the word "Life" with the outgiving of breath. Then you will become in truth the Tree of Life which sinks its roots deep into the Holy Stream of Life from an eternal source. And as the angel of sun warms the earth, and all the creatures of land and water and air rejoice in the new day, so will your body and spirit rejoice in the Holy Stream of life that flows to you through your Brother Tree.

And when the sun is high in the heavens, then shall you seek the Holy Stream of Sound. In the heat of noontide, all creatures are still and seek the shade; the angels of the Earthly Mother are silent for a space. Then it is that you shall let into your ears the Holy Stream of Sound; for it can only be heard in the silence. Think on the streams that are born in the desert after a sudden storm, and the roaring sound of the waters as they rush past. Truly, this is the voice of God, if you did but know it. For as it is written, in the beginning was the Sound, and the Sound was with God, and the Sound was God. I tell you truly, when we are born, we enter the world with the sound of God in our ears, even the singing of the vast chorus of the sky, and the holy chant of the stars in their fixed rounds; it is the Holy Stream of Sound that traverses the vault of stars and crosses the endless kingdom of the Heavenly Father. It is ever in our ears, so do we hear it not. Listen for it, then, in the silence of noontide; bathe in it, and let the rhythm of the music of God beat in your ears until you are one with the Holy Stream of Sound. It was this Sound which formed the earth and the world, and brought forth the mountains, and set the stars in their thrones of glory in the highest heavens.

And you shall bathe in the Stream of Sound, and the music of its waters shall flow over you; for in the beginning of the times so did we all share in the Holy Stream of Sound that gave birth to all creation. And the mighty roaring of the Stream of Sound will fill your whole body, and you will tremble before its might. Then breathe deeply of the angel of air, and become the sound itself, that the Holy Stream of Sound may carry you to the endless kingdom of the Heavenly Father, there where the rhythm of the world rises and falls.

And when darkness gently closes the eyes of the angels of the Earthly Mother, then shall you also sleep, that your spirit may join the unknown angels of the Heavenly Father. And in the moments before you sleep, then shall you think of the bright and glorious stars, the white, shining, far-seen and far-piercing stars. For your thoughts before sleep are as the bow of the skillful archer, that sends the arrow where he wills. Let your thoughts before sleep be with the stars; for the stars are Light, and the Heavenly Father is Light, even that Light which is a thousand times brighter than the brightness of a thousand suns. Enter the Holy Stream of Light, that the shackles of death may loose their hold for ever, and breaking free from the bonds of earth, ascend the Holy Stream of Light through the blazing radiance of the stars, into the endless kingdom of the Heavenly Father.

Unfold your wings of light, and in the eye of your thought, soar with the stars into the farthest reaches of heaven, where untold suns blaze with light. For at the beginning of the times, the Holy Law said, let there be Light, and there was Light. And you shall be one with it, and the power of the Holy Light Stream will fill your whole body, and you will tremble before its might. Say the word "Light," as you breathe deeply of the angel of air, and you will become the Light itself; and the Holy Stream will carry you to the endless kingdom of the Heavenly Father, there losing itself in the eternal Sea of Light which gives birth to all creation. And you shall be one with the Holy Stream of Light, always before you sleep in the arms of the Heavenly Father.

I tell you truly, your body was made not only to breathe, and eat, and think, but it was also made to enter the Holy Stream of Life. And your ears were made not only to hear the words of men, the song of birds, and the music of falling rain, but they were also made to hear the Holy Stream of Sound. And your eyes were made not only to see the rising and setting of the sun, the ripple of sheaves of grain, and the words of the Holy Scrolls, but they were also made to see the Holy Stream of Light. One day your body will return to the Earthly Mother; even also your ears and your eyes. But the Holy Stream of Life, the Holy Stream of Sound, and the Holy Stream of Light, these were never born, and can never die. Enter the Holy Streams, even that Life, that Sound, and that Light which gave you birth; that you may reach the kingdom of the Heavenly Father and become one with him, even as the river empties into the far-distant sea.

More than this cannot be told, for the Holy Streams will take you to that place where words are no more, and even the Holy Scrolls cannot record the mysteries therein.

CREDO
of the International Biogenic Society

We believe that our most precious possession is Life.

We believe we shall mobilize all the forces of Life against the forces of death.

We believe that mutual understanding leads toward mutual cooperation; that mutual cooperation leads toward Peace; and that Peace is the only way of survival for mankind.

We believe that we shall preserve instead of waste our natural resources, which are the heritage of our children.

We believe that we shall avoid the pollution of our air, water, and soil, the basic preconditions of Life.

We believe we shall preserve the vegetation of our planet: the humble grass which came fifty million years ago, and the majestic trees which came twenty million years ago, to prepare our planet for mankind.

We believe we shall eat only fresh, natural, pure, whole foods, without chemicals and artificial processing.

We believe we shall live a simple, natural, creative life, absorbing all the sources of energy, harmony and knowledge, in and around us.

We believe that the improvement of life and mankind on our planet must start with individual efforts, as the whole depends on the atoms composing it.

We believe in the Fatherhood of God, the Motherhood of Nature, and the Brotherhood of Man.

—composed in Paris in 1928 by Romain Rolland and Edmond Bordeaux Szekely.

APPLICATION FOR ASSOCIATE MEMBERSHIP
INTERNATIONAL BIOGENIC SOCIETY

Please return to: *I.B.S. Internacional*
                      Box 849, Nelson, B.C.
                      Canada V1L 6A5

*Name*_____

*Address*_____

*City*_____*State/Prov.*_____*Zip/Code*_____

*Age*____*Profession*_____

*Previous Experience*_____

I am interested in:

    ____*becoming an Associate Member of the I.B.S.*
    ____*becoming a Teacher of Biogenic Living.*

Enclosed is my annual Associate Membership fee of U.S. $20.00. Please mail my membership card, your current issue of the Periodical Review, *The Essene Way*, and my copy of *The Essene Way-Biogenic Living,* my "Guidebook," textbook and encyclopedia of ancient wisdom and modern practice. I understand I will receive a 20% discount on all publications as an Associate Member, but only if I order *directly* from I.B.S. Internacional.

Please make your check in U.S. currency out to
I.B.S. INTERNACIONAL.

P.S. The only reason we ask your age, profession and "previous experience" (whatever that means) is just to get to know you a little, as we may never have the chance to meet you personally. If you don't wish to answer, it's OK.

RECOMMENDED BOOKS FOR STUDY

Many members who have not yet started study groups or live far from book stores and/or like-minded individuals, are interested in a systematic program of home study. The following books are recommended for such a program, and provide an excellent foundation for study of *The Essene Way of Biogenic Living*, especially when coordinated with the methods outlined in *The Art of Study: the Sorbonne Method.*

Please send me the following books:

____*The Essene Gospel of Peace, Book One* $1.00

____*The Essene Gospel of Peace, Book Two* $7.50

____*The Essene Gospel of Peace, Book Three* $7.50

____*The Essene Gospel of Peace, Book Four* $5.95

____*The Essene Way-Biogenic Living* $8.80 *(free with membership)*

____*The Biogenic Revolution* $9.50

____*The Chemistry of Youth* $7.50

____*From Enoch to the Dead Sea Scrolls* $5.95

____*The Essene Book of Creation* $4.50

____*The Essene Code of Life* $3.50

____*The Essene Science of Life* $3.50

____*Essene Communions with the Infinite* $4.50

____*Discovery of the Essene Gospel of Peace* $5.95

____*The Essene Book of Asha* $7.50

____*Books, Our Eternal Companions* $3.50

____*Cosmos, Man and Society* $6.80

____*Search for the Ageless, Volume One* $7.80

____*Search for the Ageless, Volume Two* $8.80

____*The Ecological Health Garden, the Book of Survival* $5.95

____*The Art of Study: the Sorbonne Method* $3.50

_____*Total*

_____*Add 15% for Postage & Handling ($2.00 minimum)*

U.S. $_____*Total Amount Enclosed*

Please address all orders and correspondence to:

I.B.S. INTERNACIONAL
Box 849, Nelson, B.C., Canada V1L 6A5

Name_____

Address_____

City, State/Province, Zip/Code_____

All orders must be pre-paid. Minimum order: $10.00, minimum postage: $2.00 (foreign orders may be more). Please make check, bank draft or money order in U.S. FUNDS, drawn on a U.S. BANK, with the proper "microencoding" at the bottom of the check, out to I.B.S. INTERNACIONAL. Allow 4 weeks for processing, more for foreign orders. Members of the I.B.S. may deduct 20% and *active* Teachers of Biogenic Living may deduct 40% (both must have valid memberships for the current year). *All sales are considered final; please do not return any books.* (If there are any questions, PLEASE WRITE before acting, and please print! Dealers and distributors, write for discount information. All books have always been sent from our warehouse in the U.S., hence the necessity of payment in U.S. funds. Thank you! We send you peace and hope to hear from you soon!

CREDO
of the International Biogenic Society

We believe that our most precious possession is Life.

We believe we shall mobilize all the forces of Life against the forces of death.

We believe that mutual understanding leads toward mutal cooperation; that mutual cooperation leads toward Peace; and that Peace is the only way of survival for mankind.

We believe that we shall preserve instead of waste our natural resources, which are the heritage of our children.

We believe that we shall avoid the pollution of our air, water, and soil, the basic preconditions of Life.

We believe we shall preserve the vegetation of our planet: the humble grass which came fifty million years ago, and the majestic trees which came twenty million years ago, to prepare our planet for mankind.

We believe we shall eat only fresh, natural, pure, whole foods, without chemicals and artificial processing.

We believe we shall live a simple, natural, creative life, absorbing all the sources of energy, harmony and knowledge, in and around us.

We believe that the improvement of life and mankind on our planet must start with individual efforts, as the whole depends on the atoms composing it.

We believe in the Fatherhood of God, the Motherhood of Nature, and the Brotherhood of Man.

☐ I feel an affinity with your Credo. Please mail to me your introductory booklet, with a complete list of I.B.S. publications.

☐ I want to study the complete, all-comprehensive guidebook and encyclopedia, *The Essene Way—Biogenic Living.* I enclose my check in U.S. currency of $8.80, plus 15% for postage and handling, made out to **I.B.S. Internacional.**

☐ I want to become an Associate Member of the International Biogenic Society. My membership entitles me to receive free: (1) the comprehensive encyclopedia of ancient wisdom and modern practice, *The Essene Way—Biogenic Living,* (2) the Periodical Review of Biogenic Living, *The Essene Way,* (3) 20% discount on all publications of the I.B.S., (4) my membership card with all privileges, and (5) periodical publications. I enclose my membership fee of U.S. $20.00 (check made out to I.B.S. Internacional, renewable annually.

Please check the appropriate boxes and return this page to the International Biogenic Society, mailing address: **I.B.S. INTERNACIONAL, P.O. BOX 849, NELSON, BRITISH COLUMBIA, CANADA V1L 6A5.**

*Name*_____

*Address*_____

*City, State/Province, Zip/Code*_____

YOU MAY USE THIS FORM TO ORDER BOOKS
Please use this mailing address for all correspondence and book orders:
I.B.S. INTERNACIONAL
P.O. BOX 849, NELSON, B.C., CANADA V1L 6A5

quantity	*item*	*amount*

sub-total U.S. $_____

add 15% for postage and handling (min. $2.00 U.S. $_____

total amount enclosed (Min. order: $10.00 U.S. $_____

*Name*_____

*Address*_____

*City, State/Prov., Zip/Code*_____

Minimum order: $10.00. minimum postage & handling: $2.00 (foreign orders may be more). All orders must be prepaid. Please make check or money order (in U.S. currency, payable on a U.S. bank) out to IBS INTERNACIONAL. *Active* I.B.S. members and teachers may apply their usual discounts. Dealers and distributors, please write for discount information. Write to us at any time, we are always here (see above address). Every order is given loving attention, but ALL SALES ARE CONSIDERED FINAL.